CORNERSTONE OF NATION-BUILDING

AFRICAN AND LATINX

VOLUME TWO

Copyright © 2024 by 3D Inspirations Corp.

All rights reserved. No portion of this book may be reproduced in any form without permission from the publisher.

ISBN: 978-1-7362654-4-4

www.bernardmcarthur.com

Cornerstone of Nation-Building African and Latinx
Volume Two

First Edition

Cover and interior designed by David Ter-Avanesyan/Ter33Design LLC

CORNERSTONE OF NATION-BUILDING

AFRICAN AND LATINX

VOLUME TWO

BERNARD McARTHUR

CONTENTS

Introduction	7
GHANA	18
CUBA	54
COLUMBIA	86
BRAZIL	108
HONDURAS	132
PANAMA	142
BELIZE	154
COSTA RICA	166
ARGENTINA	176
SPAIN	188
PUERTO RICO	202
Acknowledgments	227

INTRODUCTION

While traveling to the continent of Africa and to several countries located in South America, I interviewed many Indigenous people to learn their history and get a better understanding of what life was like for their ancestors during the Transatlantic Slave Trade.

Although it was a horrific period, it is necessary to keep these stories alive. It is essential to understand how this period still affects the world today, causing financial and educational disadvantages and suppressing global competition. In this book, we will focus on the Middle Passage and the impact that the slave trade continues to have on people of African descent worldwide. Even today, a few entities outside of Africa control many natural resources and precious stones from Africa.

This book will delve into the economic impact of enslavement, how it led to the decimation of the family structure and communities, and how it continues to impact developing Latin and African nations significantly.

When studying the history of the Transatlantic Slave Trade, you will find that for hundreds of years, millions of African people were kidnapped from their homes, separated from their families, shackled with metal collars, and transported to Europe, the Americas, and the Caribbean Islands in exchange for various goods, including rum, sugar, and tobacco, and free labor. There were many names for this well-orchestrated legal human trafficking era, including the Transatlantic and Triangular Slave Trade.

The first Africans to arrive in Europe came as free people. They traded goods with European countries, owned land, and established businesses throughout the continent.

Like other cultural groups, specific African individuals embarked on journeys of exploration in pursuit of improved livelihoods. However, in the 15th century, dominant nations recognized the significance of enslaving Africans to perform unpaid labor and acquiring control over Africa's natural resources to generate substantial global wealth.

The colonizers enslaved Africans and took them from their homeland. They transported the Africans to Latin Countries, Europe, the Caribbean islands, and the Americas to create great wealth from the free labor and the control of precious natural resources in Africa. For centuries, forced labor existed in countries worldwide and was the driving force behind their economic engine and nation-building. Many enslaved people did not survive the inhumane conditions of the voyage and perished along the way. Shackled in metal chains, humans had to endure treacherous conditions on the route to a foreign world. Some individuals who refused to live a life of enslavement jumped into the shark-infested waters rather than live in captivity.

Foreigners often controlled every aspect of the enslaved people's lives. The colonizers seized land and precious metals, especially the overabundance of diamonds and gold, and forced enslaved people to work farmland and forced free labor in nation-building.

During the slave era, revolts took place worldwide, but the only country to succeed in a revolution was Haiti, leading to the emancipation of enslaved people in Haiti. During the 1800s' it was France's most profitable and prosperous European colony. Yet, Haiti became a republic and had to pay millions of francs, equivalent to billions of dollars in reparations to France for the fight for its freedom.

The process of colonization had a significant impact on Latin communities across the globe. Foreigners benefited by exploiting people of African and Afro-Latin descent, which caused great harm to these communities. The free labor of Afro-Latinos was also a crucial factor in creating immense wealth in European and Latin American countries before the advent of the Industrial Revolution.

For centuries, Afro-Latino descendants worked in fields and mines, and like what transpired in Africa, Indigenous enslaved people worked to uncover precious stones and other natural resources; however, the riches were often pilfered and taken from countries without providing any financial benefits to the natives.

After speaking to various historians from Africa, South America, and the Caribbean, I encountered related stories about the horrific treatment of enslaved people taken from their homeland and trafficked throughout Europe, the Americas, and the Caribbean.

Touring the Elmira Castle/Dungeon, W.E.B. DuBois Centre in Accra, Ghana, and speaking to historians allows one to easily imagine the horrific reality of enslavement and visualize what occurred hundreds of years ago.

It was two hours before dawn. The night was beginning to fade as the dimly lit moon illuminated the area of the small village in the middle of Ghana on the West Coast of Africa. It was a peaceful day; children played in the open field, and men went on hunts to provide food for their families. At night, elders sat around the fire telling stories passed down for generations:

The air was still humid from the earlier blazing sun and torrential downpour, with the temperature reaching well over 115 degrees and humidity at 100 %. Men were heard in the distance, praising after the successful hunt and field dressing in the scorching sun. Mothers tend to their children to ensure their bellies are full before they go to school and do their daily chores. It was the season for ceremonial rites of passage for children transitioning to adulthood.

Two months earlier, traders from Portugal landed on the shore and were amazed by the warm reception received by the African People, the beautiful landscape, and the abundance of gold worn by the elders. The locals greeted them with open arms, gave them plenty of food and water, and invited them to their homes. They brought textiles and spices, and we shared our natural resources.

Far across the ocean, the Portuguese ships traveled home after spending weeks learning about the terrain and our way of life. The Portuguese ships sailed with baskets of precious metals, gold nuggets, and heart-shaped precious stones, the people from the new land called diamonds. The locals were happy to greet them and look forward to their return.

Two months later, as the boys underwent their rites of passage and the young girls reached puberty, they would have a special ceremony, marking their transition from childhood to adulthood. The village was full of jubilation. We were even looking forward to our newfound friends' return so that we could bond with them, break bread, and take them in as if they were recently discovered family members.

Three months later, the villagers were suddenly awakened by strange and unfamiliar sounds in the middle of the night. Unlike the usual sounds of joy and sorrow from celebrations, this was an eerie and unsettling noise from mothers, children, and elderly members of the community. It was unlike anything they had heard before.

You could hear children crying and loud bangs and see flashes of fire coming from the long, narrow barrels of their rifles, followed by a sizeable black puff of smoke. There was a considerable amount of confusion throughout the village. The foreigners shot down African men as they rushed to protect their families. The colonizers shouted commands in loud voices. We recognized some of the men who had been invited to break bread with elders and were given large baskets of gifts of jewelry and precious stones to take back to their homeland. With all the confusion, they worked synchronously as if this had been rehearsed or was a customary practice in their land. The locals grabbed their machetes, which were used for multiple things: to clear the field, hunt food, and for protection in the village. The elders lay motionless on the ground, shot full of holes from the long metal pipes that spewed big puffs of smoke and fire. This was not the type of warfare with the neighboring tribes. During African warfare, captives were indoctrinated. They became valued members of the tribes, and some prisoners became tribes' leaders.

This time, it was different. Mighty, fierce warriors who had always protected the village fell to the ground, holding their chests. One minute, they were strong village leaders. The next, they lay in agony and then silence. This went on until the early morning dawn.

The following day was different. Mothers sat together, crammed in close quarters, loudly calling out for their husbands, children, babies, and elderly parents. To everyone's surprise, we were bound by metal chains and shackles. The colonizers separated us in groups from our families, from our husbands, from their protectors, and most of all, from our children. The village that had stood for centuries came crumbling down overnight. The entire town was separated by gender and age.

Men and boys were on one side, and young girls and mothers were on the other. A loud wailing pursued as babies, petrified, were taken from their mothers' arms.

The wise leaders we revered and respected, who guided us throughout life, were bound with hands behind their backs in metal shackles. The colonizers did not secure the physically challenged elderly and babies because they knew they could not make the long three-month journey through the rugged terrain to the West coast of Africa.

Why were we bound in thick iron shackles by our hands and feet, the weight of steel cutting into the skin bringing excruciating pain and anguish? These could not be the newfound friends we invited into our homes, for we treated them as village members. They brought us to our feet; men were standing next to us with long barrel rifles that made a loud noise. Shackled in chains, we walked a single line away from our homes.

We walked barefoot for months through rugged terrain, vulnerable against wild predators. In the distance, screams were heard from village members bitten by poisonous snakes, defenseless, bound by iron wrist and collar shackles, each person tied together, separated by a four-foot chain. Those bitten by toxic snakes led to a quick demise. Some said it was a better way to leave this world than to be kidnapped and taken from our homeland.

Despite enduring inhumane treatment, pain, and cries from metal bonds, we pressed on. Screams were heard not only from the metal cutting into our flesh but also from mothers because they could not hold their loved ones and did not know if they would ever see them again.

From sunrise to sunset, with little food, water, and nowhere to bathe for months, blood dripping from the heavy shackles cutting into our necks and ankles, we were forced to move on. It was like we were one extensive line of Siamese twins; when one extremity moved, the other followed in syncopation.

Sleeping on dirt at night, attracting disease-infested mosquitoes from the blood that trickled down our necks and ankles, malaria, infections from European diseases that killed and decimated many indigenous people, months of walking through the dense forest and watching our brothers, sisters, neighbors, and countless village members suffer from captivity and inhumane treatment by the captives that were once invited into our homes. We never expected this treatment from civilized nations. We lost many village members through diseases, infections, malaria, measles, mumps, chicken pox, and cruel treatments. We approached a river at the end of a three-month journey from our homes, not realizing it was a river of no return. It was our last bath on the continent of Africa.

Still in chains, we immersed ourselves in the chilly water of the river. Bathing for the first time in months, it felt like we had reached the promised land. We did not know it was the last bath before we went on a long voyage far across the ocean. We did not realize that it was the beginning of what some call purgatory.

After bathing at the riverbed, off in the distance, we saw a large white castle sitting atop the hill overlooking the sea. We saw a white fortress the colonizers called Cape Castle, one of the forty castles on the West Coast of Africa.

The first time we saw this strange home appear out of nowhere on the edge of the riverfront, we thought it would be our new home, starting a new life.

When we entered the castle grounds, we were immediately separated into groups —men, women, and children strong enough to survive the journey.

In our new home, for the next few months of confined captivity, we were taken to the bottom of the castle, which they called dungeons, devoid of sunlight. A dark section cut out of the white stone, no sunlight, and the smell of death lingering in the air. It was the final resting place for many of the enslaved Africans. The putrid smell of decaying bodies, the stench from human waste, blood, and airborne diseases easily passed quickly to humans crammed into small holding cells, still shackled in chains, with little space to stand, bodies touching the person next to you with swollen body parts infected from the wrought iron on their wrist and ankles. Our women endured similar harsh treatment.

The Africans that tried to revolt were quickly separated and put in a small stone room with little ventilation and no food or water, left to die. It was an impactful message of fear. Each person removed individually from the dungeon rarely returned.

The dungeon echoed with moans and cries, leaving us unsure if we would ever see daylight.

Some enslaved Africans who survived months in darkness confined in dungeons with little food or water lost sight.

When the Guineamen ships arrived for the human trafficking across the Atlantic Ocean, we were led against our will to the courtyard to walk through the door of no return. We realized our life in Africa had ended, and we would never return to Africa.

They boarded us quickly, a bountiful harvest for some and a life of bondage transported across the Atlantic Ocean, shackled, stacked on top of each other with little room separating us. We lay flat without space to sit up so the captives could transport as much of a load of enslaved Africans as possible to new lands worldwide to provide free labor for the colonizers. Most of the enslaved Africans that were kidnapped from Africa were taken to Latin countries.

When ships arrived, enslaved Africans were quickly removed from the dungeons and passed through *"the door of no return"* to start the journey of the middle passage by colonizers.

Ships arrived from all over Europe and the Americas; Duncan, Duc du Maine, Aurore, and numerous other cargo ships converted to human trafficking ships transported enslaved human cargo in Europe, South America, North America, Central America, and the Caribbean islands.

This book was one of the most challenging projects I have ever undertaken. Researching, documenting, and photographing the atrocities that Africans and Afro-Latino people endured from the 15th through the 19th century was heart-wrenching. As I traveled to each country featured in the book, I could not help but see the lasting impact of enslaving these people and their ancestors who provided free labor for hundreds of years, many of whom still live in poverty today.

Ghana was the first African country to gain independence from a world superpower, Great Britain. When the first European Portuguese invaded the country in 1497, they found so much gold that they called Ghana the Gold Coast. Colonizers throughout Europe and the Americas enslaved and controlled the African continent for hundreds of years.

After the abolition of slavery, enslaved individuals had to start their lives from scratch with limited financial resources, inadequate education, and housing. They were often unskilled in the new labor force. Some of the formerly enslaved individuals were compelled to work as indentured servants and were paid low wages, which were barely enough to support their families. Despite centuries of inhumane treatment, communities that have suffered and had so much taken from their land continue to live and work in impoverished conditions.

It is surprising to think that despite the great wealth established around the world from African and Afro-Latino enslavement, countries did not receive adequate compensation for the free human labor, precious metals, diamonds, gold, and other natural resources that were taken from their land. This exploitation contributed to building hyperpower nations but did not benefit the developing countries from which the resources were taken. If even a small percentage of this wealth were reinvested in these developing nations, it would help reduce people's need to emigrate and seek a better life in other countries. African and Afro-Latino descendants continue to endure vast hardships throughout the world.

This book will shed light on the blending of Black and Latino people that makes the world so beautiful. African culture is passed down from generation to generation through various methods, and its influence is celebrated worldwide.

For centuries, people of African and Afro-Latino descent have faced numerous challenges, including living in deprived communities, attending inferior schools, lacking access to medical attention, residing in depleted neighborhoods, and suffering from psychological trauma caused by centuries of inhumane conditions around the world. However, their resilience has allowed them to achieve remarkable accomplishments globally in business and academic success. Despite the complex obstacles that individuals face, they have proven that reaching the highest levels of success is possible with the right opportunities. Sonia Sotomayor, a Supreme Court Justice, is a living example of this achievement.

This book is a journey across continents. It includes photographs of the enslavement trail in African and Latin communities. In addition, it shows the blended cultures of Black and Brown people and countries that have accepted and embraced the many fine things that have come out of Africa and are woven into the fabric of society.

The music, culture, food, dance, and nation-building are prevalent throughout the Western Hemisphere. Some cultural traditions date back hundreds of years.

Over the years, numerous studies have been conducted on the economic and psychological impact of the Middle Passage. When you travel to countries with a high Afro-Latino population because of enslaved communities, you will notice economic disparities between the countries that benefited from a horrific period in world history.

African and Afro-Latino descendants contributed to every aspect of humanity's evolution, from salt mines to gold mines, healthcare, inventions, and construction. The enslaved people also fought wars for the rights to freedom, liberty, and justice.

There is a clear divide in terms of the economy, psychology, and deprivation of impoverished neighborhoods in African and Afro-Latino countries, which can be traced back to the enslavement of these communities. Before emancipation, indoctrination led to the belief that the color of one's skin made them inferior in society. Today, many people still live in deplorable economic conditions and aspire to provide a better life for their families and achieve prosperity.

Many governments use imperial relationships to rule and control countries and people. They claim foreign land and the country's natural resources as locals continue indentured servitude. Countries are indebted to superpowers and strong financial nations between building infrastructure and providing humanitarian relief. With the current technological advantages, superpower countries that benefited from enslaving people continue to control the money supply and are driving down Gross Domestic Products with innovative technological productivity gains. It makes it difficult for emerging African and Latino communities to compete globally. As they fall further behind, one wonders what the outlook for the future will be.

How will the smaller nations fair globally when you look at the fast-moving technological gains and scientific research shared with superpower nations? Artificial Intelligence and robotics are very costly and efficient forms of production. How will developing countries be considered in the equation of shared technology and global competition?

On a global scale, it is not easy to be competitive when countries amass great wealth from the free labor of enslaved people who built and provided financial advantages. The wealth derived from free work and resources taken from countries should be factorized into the economic equation for emerging countries.

Especially when colonizers continued to claim precious metals, land, and resources for hundreds of years, slavery transformed many countries into economic powerhouses. From the financial gains derived from such countries, there should be a responsibility to share technological, medical, and scientific research with emerging nations.

Today, many people try to escape the pillaged communities and establish a new life in a country that built great wealth from their free labor.

When you travel to different countries, you quickly become aware of the differences in financial wealth and income inequality.

Superpower nations should share technological advancements with African and Afro-Latino countries that have significantly built powerful nations. We can learn from our past to have a better future in all countries. Our world is a blend of mixed cultures with similar values and needs. Unfortunately, many children are still malnourished and die of starvation and diseases that have already been eradicated in superpower countries. A lack of medical care makes survival a struggle in parts of South America, Central America, Caribbean islands, and African villages.

Many countries are falling behind economically and technologically. Automation, robotics, and artificial intelligence replace human involvement in merging nations. As a nation, we must take the lead to share the wealth so voluntarily or involuntarily families are not forced to uproot households in search of a better life.

GHANA

The nation of Ghana played a pivotal part in the transatlantic slave trade. When Europeans first arrived, they traded in gold; however, they soon realized enslaving Africans was more profitable. The colonizers transported over ten million enslaved people from West Africa to the Americas, Europe, and the Caribbean. On the coast of Ghana, over forty castles confined enslaved people in dungeons for months before being transported to Europe, South America, North America, and the Caribbean islands.

Before the era of enslaving Africans, Ghanaian explorers welcomed foreigners into their villages and traded gold and other precious metals for European goods as early as the 1400s. In 1957, Ghana finally became a Republic.

Foreigners continued to control land confiscated in the 1500s. In the past, gold was obtained from mines and flowed downstream. Soon after, they realized enslaving Ghanaians was more profitable than trading gold.

Ghana is a peaceful nation invaded by Portugal, the Netherlands, England, and the Americas. Despite this history of violence and exploitation, Ghana has been able to forgive and move on from the dreadful, brutal, and inhumane aspects of enslaving Black Africans.

Today, Ghana is one of the largest cocoa producers in the world. The plants grow within the country, but they do not have the technology to process cocoa plants. Ghana only receives a small percentage of profits from its rich agricultural plants. From fishing villages to the industrial city of Accra, you can still see the devastating economic impact of enslaving people.

Over 80% of Ghanaians practice Christianity during its long, insightful history. A country still called the Gold Coast because of its abundant gold and other rich natural resources throughout its land has suffered inhumanely. During the slave trade era, its people were incited to go to war by outsiders. Its ancestors were enslaved, treated as chattel, and deemed less than human.

Ghana and other African countries continue to be indebted to foreign countries for building their infrastructure and processing their natural resources, cocoa, oil, and lithium. The wealth generated by natural resources has been exploited, and the government remains indebted to foreign powers.

BERNARD McARTHUR

CORNERSTONE OF NATION-BUILDING: AFRICAN AND LATINX

CORNERSTONE OF NATION-BUILDING: AFRICAN AND LATINX

CORNERSTONE OF NATION-BUILDING: AFRICAN AND LATINX

CORNERSTONE OF NATION-BUILDING: AFRICAN AND LATINX

CORNERSTONE OF NATION-BUILDING: AFRICAN AND LATINX

CORNERSTONE OF NATION-BUILDING: AFRICAN AND LATINX

CUBA

Cuba played a significant role in the Transatlantic Slave Trade, with sugar, rice, tobacco, and coffee being the main products exported from the country. Cuba was Spain's colony in the Caribbean for hundreds of years until around the 19th century, when America helped Cuba gain independence from Spain. In 1959, Fidel Castro and Ernesto Che Guevara led a Cuban revolution.

When Fidel Castro became president, he abolished segregation policies and vowed to end racism in Cuba. He initiated policies to end discrimination and established that Black and White people were equal before the law. At the time of the revolution, most Cubans were illiterate. Castro's government instilled nationalism, where everyone had to go to school, and the Cuban people also had access to medical care.

In 1962, The United States imposed an economic trade embargo on Cuba, which remains in effect today. Despite the blockade, the Cuban Revolution achieved its healthcare, education, and sovereignty goals. It is important to note that the Cuban government has a considerable influence on the everyday lives of its citizens.

At the collapse of the Soviet Union, Cuba endured severe economic hardship for over 60 years.

Along with food shortages in Cuba, medical supplies, electricity, and other commodities are in short supply. It is remarkable to see the Cuban citizens deprived of necessities yet still achieving significant advancements in medicine, engineering, and law. Even with limited medication and an abundant world supply of antibiotics because of the embargo, the country has a limited supply of drugs. In Cuba, healthcare is available to all residents. Cuban doctors have provided medical assistance to developing nations, particularly after natural disasters, since the 1960s.

Most of Cuba's population is of African and European mixed-race ancestry. During Cuba's battle history, at one time, it was led by an Afro-Cuban General and political leader, Antoni Maceo, during the war of independence from Spain. Afro-Cuban music and dance is an integral part of their culture. Many renowned jazz musicians travel to Cuba to experience it.

Santiago has a substantial Afro-Cuban diversity, and music studios, museums, and restaurants are throughout the city. It is now a country free from colonialism.

CORNERSTONE OF NATION-BUILDING: AFRICAN AND LATINX

CORNERSTONE OF NATION-BUILDING: AFRICAN AND LATINX

CORNERSTONE OF NATION-BUILDING: AFRICAN AND LATINX

BERNARD McARTHUR

CORNERSTONE OF NATION-BUILDING: AFRICAN AND LATINX

CORNERSTONE OF NATION-BUILDING: AFRICAN AND LATINX

CORNERSTONE OF NATION-BUILDING: AFRICAN AND LATINX

CORNERSTONE OF NATION-BUILDING: AFRICAN AND LATINX

CORNERSTONE OF NATION-BUILDING: AFRICAN AND LATINX

CORNERSTONE OF NATION-BUILDING: AFRICAN AND LATINX

COLOMBIA

Enslaved Africans were transported to Colombia from the beginning of the 16th century until its definitive abolition in 1851. This process consisted of the trafficking of people of African and Indigenous origin, first by the European colonizers from Spain and later by the commercial elites of the Republic of New Granada. This country contained what is present-day Colombia. Spanish conquerors subjected Indigenous peoples to forced labor and other abuses.

Medellin is indeed a city rich in cultural heritage. Culture and arts are a must-see in Medellin, along with beautiful landscapes. Its roots are deeply entrenched in blending various Indigenous cultures. The city has made great strides in transitioning from agriculture of coca plants and drug trafficking to an art and culture community. The city is adorned with sculptures by the renowned artist Fernando Botero. The cultural heritage of Medellin is beautifully displayed through its many museums, galleries, and lively street art scenes. The city is also known for its beautiful landscapes, which visitors must see.

The city of Cartagena de Indias in Colombia served as the port for the disembarkation of enslaved people from the West Coast of Africa. The enslaved Indigenous people were separated so that individuals of the same ethnicity or region were not together. Enslaved Africans were exhibited outdoors and sold at the Plaza de Los Coches. In addition to labor in the fields, owning enslaved people was a status symbol of prosperous Spaniards in Cartagena. During the 17th century, enslaved Africans were traded for 200-400 silver pesos each.

Today, Cartagena is a breathtaking colonial architectural city in Colombia. It is an exclusive tourist vacation haven. At any time, you can see horse-drawn carriages throughout the city. The town's stone wall defended against British and other invasions.

CORNERSTONE OF NATION-BUILDING: AFRICAN AND LATINX

CORNERSTONE OF NATION-BUILDING: AFRICAN AND LATINX

CORNERSTONE OF NATION-BUILDING: AFRICAN AND LATINX

CORNERSTONE OF NATION-BUILDING: AFRICAN AND LATINX

CORNERSTONE OF NATION-BUILDING: AFRICAN AND LATINX

BRAZIL

Brazil has a long and complex history of enslaving Africans. The importation of enslaved Africans: During the Atlantic Slave Trade, Brazil imported more Africans than any other country.

Many enslaved Africans worked in tobacco, sugar cane, coffee fields, and gold mines. The enslaved Black Africans were not as susceptible to infectious European diseases as Indigenous natives in Brazil; many perished because they did not have immunity to European diseases. The enslaved Black Africans outnumbered Brazilians at one point in time.

Brazil has a rich African history. Millions of people defined themselves as having Black African or mixed-race ancestry. For hundreds of centuries, free labor provided by Black Africans in tobacco, sugar cane, and other industries made many people very wealthy. However, there is a staggering economic gap between rich and impoverished Brazilians. There has been significant headway in assisting individuals in breaking free from poverty and favelas. Yet still, for a country that has an exceedingly high percentage of its citizens living in poverty, they are perceived as looking at life not from their economic conditions but from a place of pride and unity.

CORNERSTONE OF NATION-BUILDING: AFRICAN AND LATINX

BERNARD McARTHUR

CORNERSTONE OF NATION-BUILDING: AFRICAN AND LATINX

CORNERSTONE OF NATION-BUILDING: AFRICAN AND LATINX

CORNERSTONE OF NATION-BUILDING: AFRICAN AND LATINX

HONDURAS

Honduras was a Spanish colony. The Lencas lived in the western-central part of Honduras, while the Tol occupied the central north coast. The Pech (or Paya), Maya, and Sumo lived east and west of Trujillo.

African slavery was introduced into Honduras in 1545 due to the Spanish conquest.

Enslaved Africans were transported to Honduras to work in the mining sector. Most Hondurans are a mixed race of Spanish and Mestizos. Around 2% of the Hondurans are of African descent. Honduras is a country located in Central America that faces significant challenges in terms of development and safety.

CORNERSTONE OF NATION-BUILDING: AFRICAN AND LATINX

PANAMA

Panama was a significant distribution point for enslaved people transported to other parts of the country. Between the casualties of war and diseases from the outside world, the Cimarrons in Panama were enslaved Africans who abandoned their Spanish masters in the mid-16th century. When brought to Panama, they intermarried with the natives and immediately learned the land to outsmart the Spanish. An estimated 3,000 of them lived in Nombre de Dios, a town on the Caribbean side.

Thousands of enslaved Africans fled captivity in Spanish Panama from the 1520s through the 1580s and formed their communities. These communities were self-sufficient and periodically raided Spanish settlements. The self-governance of these communities incited armed conflict as Spaniards sought to conquer them and kill or re-enslave their populations. Through persistent rebellion, these enslaved people gained their freedom and self-governance, which is significant. It is an anomaly because it was during the harshest periods of the Transatlantic Slave Trade that individuals of African descent found ways to resist enslavement, secure their autonomy, organize those communities, and lead rebellions.

Panama is an ethnic melting pot of the Central Caribbean, and one of the largest ethnic groups is African descent. The ingenuity of scientists and working people constructed one of the world's marvels, the Panama Canal, completed in 1914. Over 10,000 ships pass through the Panama Canal annually. Significant sacrifices were made in building the Panama Canal, and many locals lost their lives. The treacherous terrain, malaria, and mishaps during construction caused many deaths.

CORNERSTONE OF NATION-BUILDING: AFRICAN AND LATINX

CORNERSTONE OF NATION-BUILDING: AFRICAN AND LATINX

CORNERSTONE OF NATION-BUILDING: AFRICAN AND LATINX

CORNERSTONE OF NATION-BUILDING: AFRICAN AND LATINX

BELIZE

Belize has a complex history of colonization and slavery. It was once a colony of both Spain and the British. The earliest reference to enslaved Africans in Belize can be traced back to enslaved individuals from various British colonies, including Jamaica and Bermuda, who were exported there in the 18th century.

Belize has a diverse population consisting of individuals with Mestizo, Spanish, and Indigenous ancestry.

This country is home to the world's largest jaguar sanctuary, which protects the jaguar in wildlife sanctuaries to ensure its survival.

CORNERSTONE OF NATION-BUILDING: AFRICAN AND LATINX

CORNERSTONE OF NATION-BUILDING: AFRICAN AND LATINX

BERNARD McARTHUR

CORNERSTONE OF NATION-BUILDING: AFRICAN AND LATINX

COSTA RICA

The initial enslaved Africans were transported to Costa Rica from Spain, and they had a significant impact on the country's development and culture. Over 12% of the population is of African descent. Costa Rica gained its independence from Spain in 1812. Nowadays, many American expatriates reside in Costa Rica due to the affordable cost of living and medical care.

Costa Rica is also famous for its rich biodiversity. Most of the country's land is rural, providing an ideal habitat for various exotic birds and wildlife, making it a bird watcher's paradise. Additionally, Costa Rica is renowned for its animal refuges. The country possesses over one hundred biological reserves and fifty wildlife refuges, contributing to its reputation as a conservation-focused nation.

CORNERSTONE OF NATION-BUILDING: AFRICAN AND LATINX

CORNERSTONE OF NATION-BUILDING: AFRICAN AND LATINX

CORNERSTONE OF NATION-BUILDING: AFRICAN AND LATINX

ARGENTINA

Many Indigenous tribes once inhabited Argentina. The first Europeans arrived in the 16th century when Spain colonized the country. Foreign diseases wiped out most of the Indigenous people of Argentina. After the demise of many Indigenous ethnic groups, enslaved people from Africa were brought to Argentina, and they became known as Afro-Argentines. The first enslaved people arrived in Buenos Aires from Brazil around 1587, and the main commercial activity for Buenos Aires was the slave trade. Enslaved people came primarily to Argentina by Portuguese slave traders. Portuguese also transported enslaved people to Peru (Lima), Chile, Bolivia, and southern Peru. By the mid-17th century, religious orders brought enslaved Africans to labor on ranches, universities, and churches.

In 1810, enslaved Africans fought for Argentine independence in securing their freedom. The participation of enslaved people initiated the Free Womb Act, which "freed" all babies born to slave mothers. In 1861, slavery was abolished entirely in Argentina.

CORNERSTONE OF NATION-BUILDING: AFRICAN AND LATINX

CORNERSTONE OF NATION-BUILDING: AFRICAN AND LATINX

CORNERSTONE OF NATION-BUILDING: AFRICAN AND LATINX

SPAIN

Spain has a rich history of exploration and colonization and is known for its global influence. During the 15th century, Spain began trading enslaved people, and this trade reached its peak in the 16th century. In the mid-1400s, Portuguese slave traders began to operate in Seville, Spain. Spaniards enslaved many Africans to work in the agricultural fields in the Caribbean. Slavery was also prevalent among Native Americans in both Mesoamerica and South America. The Spanish conquistadors were a powerful part of Spain's expansion. They were partly responsible for colonizing much of South America and Mexico.

Hannibal once ruled Spain. He was a Carthaginian general who fought against Rome in the Second Punic War.

CORNERSTONE OF NATION-BUILDING: AFRICAN AND LATINX

CORNERSTONE OF NATION-BUILDING: AFRICAN AND LATINX

BERNARD McARTHUR

CORNERSTONE OF NATION-BUILDING: AFRICAN AND LATINX

PUERTO RICO

Before the Spanish invasion in 1493, the Taino people were the dominant culture in Puerto Rico. After colonization, the Indigenous people were enslaved, and their population drastically declined due to European diseases. In the 1500s, Puerto Rico and Cuba were colonies of Spain. Enslaved Africans were brought to Puerto Rico and the Caribbean islands to work the tobacco and sugar cane fields. Puerto Rico played a significant role in Spain's economy. San Juan Bay constructed a massive Fort, San Felipe del Morro, to protect Puerto Rico's Bay.

During the Spanish-American war, Puerto Rico became a United States territory under the Treaty of Paris. A sizable percentage of the Puerto Rican heritage was of Black African ancestry. The overwhelming majority of trade is between the United States. During that period, the United States invested heavily in the infrastructure and education of Puerto Rican citizens. Puerto Rico is considered a Commonwealth of the United States.

Around 1950, Puerto Rico shifted from an agricultural producer to an industrial economy. Many manufacturers relocated operations to Puerto Rico.

For many years, Puerto Rico forged a relationship with Cuba. Their flags are similar. After the Cuban Revolution, Puerto Rico severed ties with Cuba.

CORNERSTONE OF NATION-BUILDING: AFRICAN AND LATINX

Today, a blended bloodline, Puerto Rico has evolved by mixing Spanish, African, Caribbean, and Taino Indian Indigenous peoples. Its pristine beaches and mountainous and forested areas extend its beauty throughout each side of Puerto Rico, a US territory.

CORNERSTONE OF NATION-BUILDING: AFRICAN AND LATINX

BERNARD McARTHUR

CORNERSTONE OF NATION-BUILDING: AFRICAN AND LATINX

CORNERSTONE OF NATION-BUILDING: AFRICAN AND LATINX

CORNERSTONE OF NATION-BUILDING: AFRICAN AND LATINX

CORNERSTONE OF NATION-BUILDING: AFRICAN AND LATINX

ACKNOWLEDGMENTS

I want to dedicate this book to the determination and resilient mothers who have been the backbone of our diaspora. Despite the pain, suffering, and disappointment they have faced, they remain the foundation of our society. Their resilience, tenacity, resolve, and strength have carried us through the centuries. They continue to support us until we can stand on our own. When we stumble, they are there to catch us; when we are broken, they help us heal. They have been the reason we have come so far, and we love and revere them for all they have given and continue to give to make this world a better place. The cradle of civilization rests on their shoulders, and we thank them.

I would also like to express my gratitude to some unique individuals who have always provided love, support, and unwavering devotion to our family. Firstly, I want to acknowledge my sister-in-law, Sakina Abdul Haqq, and her mother, Jeanette Bey, for their continuous support of the family and community development. Next is Melvina Robinson, our mother's closest friend and relative. She comes from a family with roots extending from Panama to Harlem, New York. She was my mother's closest friend and relative, and we always cherished the memories we shared with her. Of course, I cannot forget to mention our mother, Elizabeth Reily-Murrain-Galloway-McArthur, whose family extends from Long Ground, Montserrat, throughout New York City. Additionally, I would like to mention our loving sisters, Eleanor, Jean, Arlanna, Debra, and Bernice. They provided us with so much love after we lost our mother at an early age and filled the gap for so many years. Lastly, I want to express my gratitude to my mother-in-law, Virginia Kinard, a strong and independent woman who played a significant role in raising our daughters.

Growing up in a close-knit community during the turbulent Civil Rights Era, specific individuals played a significant role in our development. These matriarchs provided guidance and insights about life and were present throughout the most influential years of our lives. Although it is impossible to list them all, we are immensely grateful for the love and support they have given us. Arlene McArthur, Dr. Doris Banks Henries, Mary Young, Martha McArthur, Barbara Ann Davis, Edith Holloman, Betty Thomas, Rosa Harvey, Ruby Shelton, Fannie Rankins Privott, Alice Rankins-Privott, Salmon Wright Clara Vereen, Lila Snipes, Celestine Vereen, Margaret Bivens, Hattie Wright, Florence Perry, Catherine Ezell, Rutner Hilton, Bertha Bush, Edith Barnes, Barbara Roam, Cheryl Clarke, Esmeralda Amritt, Dr. Reverend Ethel Banks Graham, Mary Marshall, Deloris Gaunichaux, Julia Brown, Barbara Sneed, Bea Lockhart, and Eloise Hart.

Sankofa
"Know your past and go forward in the future."

www.ingramcontent.com/pod-product-compliance
Lightning Source LLC
Chambersburg PA
CBHW080611100526
44585CB00035B/2321